THE 12 TRIBES CHART

COLORING ACTIVITY BOOK

12 Tribes Of Israel

Judah - American Blacks

Benjamin - West Indian Blacks

Levi - Haitians

Ephraim - Puerto Ricans

Manasseh - Cubans

Simeon - Dominicans

Zebulon - Guatemala to Panama (Mayans)

Gad - Native-American Indians

Reuben - Seminole Indians

Asher - Columbia to Uruguay (Incas)

Issachar - Mexicans (Aztecs)

Naphtali - Argentina/Chile

The Promised Land was divided among the twelve tribes of Israel.

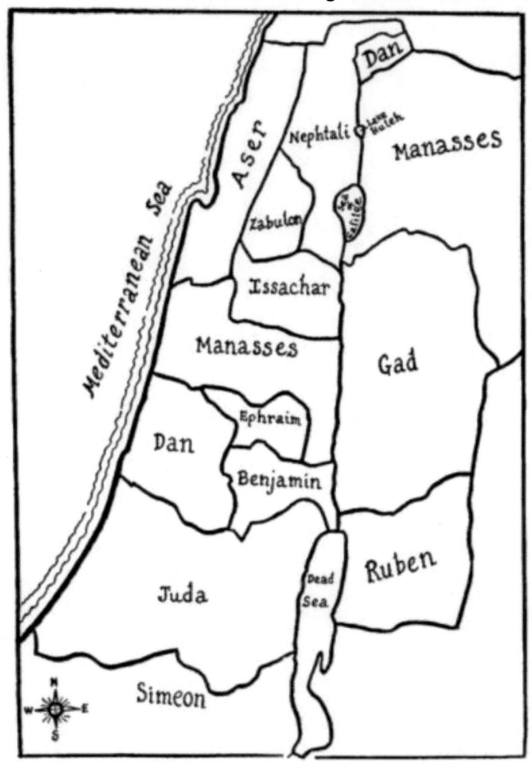

MATCH UP THE CORRECT TRIBE TO THEIR SO-CALLED NAMES.

1.	JUDAH	a. GUATEMALA TO PANAMA
2.	BENJAMIN	b. AMERICAN BLACK
3.	LEVI	c. PUERTO RICANS
4.	EPHRAIM	d. ARGENTINA
5.	MANASSEH	e. COLUMBIA TO URUGUAY
6.	SIMEON	f. NATIVE AMERICAN INDIANS
7.	ZEBULON	g. MEXICANS
8.	GAD	h. CUBANS
9.	REUBEN	i. WEST INDIAN BLACKS
10.	ASHER	j. SEMINOLE INDIANS
11.	ISSACHAR	k. HAITIANS
12.	NAPHTALI	l. DOMINICANS

BENJAMIN

Benjamin, was the twelfth son of Jacob. His name means "Son of the Right".

UNSCRAMBLE THE 12 TRIBES

1. LEIV

2. NBREUE

3. NAJEMINB

4. MIPHREA

5. HATNLIAP

6. HERSA

7. AUJDH

8. SMONEI

9. BZOLENU

10. GDA

11. CIAHRSSA

12. SAASMHNE

Judah

Location: North America and scattered, regions of the Earth.

Deuteronomy 28:68 - ⁶⁸ And the LORD shall bring thee into Egypt again with ships, by the way whereof I spake unto thee, Thou shalt see it no more again: and there ye shall be sold unto your enemies for bondmen and bondwomen, and no man shall buy you.

Judah

GAD

Gad migrated to the Americans around 536 B>C during the Persian captivity.

FLASHCARDS

1 JUDAH/PRAISE	**7** 1 CORINTHIANS 6:7
2 REUBEN/SEE A SON	**8** 1 CORINTHIANS 3:5-9
3 GAD/A TROOP	**9** MATTHEW 6:33 - ACTS 2:41,47
4 NAPHTALI/WRESTLING	**10** PSALMS 45:10
5 ASHER/BLESSED OR HAPPY	**11** DEUTERONOMY 33:12
6 SIMEON/HEARING	**12** GENESIS 41:52

FLASHCARD

FLASHCARD

LEVI/JOINED	GENESIS 29:35
ISSACHAR/HIRE	GENESIS 29:32
ZEBULUN/DWELLING	ROM 11:25
MANASSEH/FORGETTING	EPHESIANS 6:12
BENJAMN/SON OF MY RIGHT HAND	PSALMS 144:15
EPHRAIM/FRUITFUL	JOHN 10:3

FLASH CARD

GAD

GAD was the seventh born son of Jacob. His Name means "Troop". The word Indian comes from the Latin word "Indio" meaning slave.

LEVI

Genesis 49:5 - [5] Simeon and Levi are brethren; instruments of cruelty are in their habitations.

```
W  O  A  O  S  K  U  F  S  P  R  L  H  S  Z  B  L  L  D  Z
C  I  T  U  V  C  N  R  Y  X  T  S  F  M  O  P  B  G  U  Q
R  V  X  A  Y  P  A  A  N  G  Q  O  N  V  Y  N  U  U  E  P
U  P  Q  R  H  D  C  T  D  R  V  S  J  A  C  O  B  T  G  P
E  F  G  M  W  R  G  V  T  L  B  S  Z  N  I  R  R  J  D  C
L  S  V  K  Y  N  Q  C  E  E  Y  X  I  O  Q  T  L  B  Z  Z
T  O  Y  Z  Z  R  G  V  K  G  R  K  T  I  T  H  I  B  C  K
Y  G  U  P  U  B  I  B  X  Y  O  E  I  T  Z  S  T  A  X  G
D  I  Y  B  J  Y  N  E  H  Z  V  N  D  A  T  N  Z  G  H  P
G  Q  A  V  D  J  W  A  H  Q  S  D  A  T  S  I  M  E  O  N
E  H  B  F  N  R  Y  B  Z  T  E  W  V  I  A  W  D  N  E  S
A  N  Q  C  I  R  P  M  R  N  E  R  V  B  Z  L  J  R  V  X
R  X  O  R  D  J  R  U  I  C  R  D  Q  A  K  I  H  Y  D  R
T  S  G  J  L  U  M  O  P  V  E  C  V  H  D  T  B  Y  K  O
H  N  P  A  P  E  J  N  A  I  W  Y  D  J  E  E  G  B  L  L
N  G  G  E  N  E  S  I  S  W  H  M  O  R  A  A  R  P  M  C
W  X  T  T  R  S  C  W  J  Z  E  S  B  X  K  W  J  G  Y  P
D  F  S  Q  T  H  X  Q  H  S  B  A  R  E  G  I  O  N  S  X
W  I  P  O  K  N  B  N  N  Q  Z  E  L  I  L  L  M  A  T  L
X  F  G  D  I  M  S  S  D  Q  O  E  C  W  E  M  V  T  G  H
```

LEVI	HAITIANS	SCATTERED
REGIONS	EARTH	JOINED
SON	JACOB	GENESIS
SIMEON	BRETHREN	INSTRUMENTS
CRUELTY	THEIR	HABITATION

GAD

Deuteronomy 33:20 - [20] And of Gad he said, Blessed be he that enlargeth Gad: he dwelleth as a lion, and teareth the arm with the crown of the head.

REUBEN

Genesis 29:32 - [32] **And Leah conceived, and bare a son, and she called his name Reuben: for she said, Surely the LORD hath looked upon my affliction; now therefore my husband will love .**

```
T  L  O  Q  L  E  A  H  A  D  H  Z  R  P  M  P  N  I  R  Y
M  A  N  D  K  X  T  D  T  I  R  S  O  O  O  B  R  V  H  Y
A  H  X  V  M  D  T  Y  E  R  B  G  G  D  L  P  O  O  U  V
W  Z  C  Q  S  Y  D  W  M  Q  I  V  E  Q  E  J  B  C  W  R
Y  S  P  N  H  N  G  D  U  R  C  F  N  L  J  Q  E  L  A  Y
G  E  N  A  A  N  A  U  R  E  U  B  E  N  O  D  H  B  S  J
W  R  E  B  Y  U  F  I  R  Y  H  K  S  M  W  N  L  E  C  F
O  E  S  Y  H  U  I  W  D  M  I  N  I  O  Z  M  I  G  L  T
Y  U  M  V  A  D  Z  W  R  N  N  J  S  N  O  K  A  M  A  Y
H  K  F  D  A  F  Y  T  Y  Z  I  D  Y  T  A  U  R  F  E  Y
H  K  A  I  S  N  C  R  G  H  J  B  I  C  U  I  F  Q  T  S
O  E  Y  C  T  B  G  B  H  K  A  I  E  A  C  L  E  Q  D  O
D  E  V  I  E  C  N  O  C  R  P  H  I  D  I  C  O  J  F  W
R  G  M  F  J  Y  W  X  X  S  M  F  N  C  P  H  A  R  I  A
L  O  J  W  O  E  F  L  L  F  V  O  T  T  R  I  O  C  D  Q
Z  K  C  Y  R  W  P  J  M  B  Y  I  R  H  S  C  U  M  P  Z
R  S  X  J  U  L  O  C  X  A  O  I  P  P  P  O  E  E  U  O
R  U  Q  N  Z  S  S  J  A  N  C  Y  K  L  C  Y  N  V  C  G
D  M  L  I  T  Z  K  K  M  X  R  Z  E  W  O  Y  H  U  M  N
J  W  V  L  T  U  U  I  F  B  A  J  N  E  A  N  X  C  K
```

REUBEN	SEMINOLE	MUSKOGEE
INDIANS	FIRTH	BORN
SON	JACOB	GENESIS
CONCEIVED	LORD	HUSBAND
AFFLICTION	LEAH	

1 Chronicles 5:18- ¹⁸ The sons of Reuben, and the Gadites, and half the tribe of Manasseh, of valiant men, men able to bear buckler and sword, and to shoot with bow, and skilful in war, were four and forty thousand seven hundred and threescore, that went out to the war.

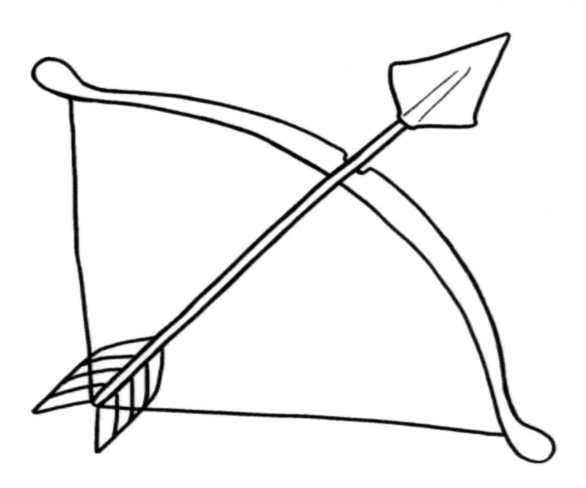

FILL IN THE BLANKS

2 ESDRAS 13:40-45

1. Those are the ten _____ which were carried away _____ out of |their own land in the time of _____ the king, whom _____ the king of _____

2. Led away _____ and he carried them over the _____ and so came they into another land.

3. But they took this _____ among themselves, that they would leave the _____ of the _____ and go forth into a further country, where never _____ dwelt,

4. That they might there keep their _____ which they never kept in their own _____

5. And they entered into _____ by the narrow places of the river.

6. For the most High then shewed _____ for them, and held still the _____ till they were passed over.

7. For _____ that country there was a great way to go, _____ of a year and a half: and the same region is called

land. Assyria waters, tribes, through mankind signs multitude counsel prisoners Osea flood, Euphrates Arsareth. namely, Salmanasar heathen, statutes, captive,

BENJAMIN

Along with Judah and Levi, Benjamin was sold into captivity (By the Africans and the Arabs) to the white man. The white man then transported them in chains on slave ships to Jamaica, and various West Indian islands to serve hard bondage as slaves.

EPHRAIM

Hosea 7:8 - [8] **Ephraim, he hath mixed himself among the people; Ephraim is a cake not turned.**

ASHER

Genesis 30:13 - ¹³ **And Leah said, Happy am I, for the daughters will call me blessed: and she called his name Asher.**

```
Y  T  F  E  O  Q  H  M  A  R  B  V  I  A  D  X  Q  J  C  H
H  T  C  Y  F  B  A  F  V  W  L  E  A  H  A  T  E  R  U  F
X  E  C  J  X  Q  B  N  I  P  G  A  X  N  R  R  U  B  K  Y
J  H  B  L  M  L  A  R  E  F  K  E  E  I  G  H  T  H  C  S
A  M  G  V  E  J  J  I  T  E  B  W  M  E  K  X  A  G  D  F
C  F  R  S  G  O  E  E  B  X  J  B  Z  H  R  H  R  P  X  C
O  P  S  A  Z  W  I  R  U  M  S  Q  C  B  X  F  E  Y  P  Z
B  E  K  W  S  J  Q  B  B  Z  O  K  I  F  V  Q  D  L  P  Y
D  R  C  O  A  K  F  Q  O  G  N  L  A  M  C  R  A  P  B  I
S  U  U  W  L  Q  B  P  R  D  W  I  O  O  G  V  U  I  Y  M
I  T  M  C  C  I  Y  G  B  L  X  A  X  C  R  A  G  X  M  S
H  F  Q  X  O  O  Z  N  T  U  S  S  W  V  H  B  H  W  X  S
F  U  M  H  C  T  R  A  V  E  X  H  Y  U  A  J  T  B  R  E
O  T  C  X  I  G  M  C  R  R  O  E  G  L  P  M  E  F  X  O
C  W  F  Y  K  C  P  I  J  B  O  R  Y  S  K  E  R  P  D  X
X  C  J  M  U  Z  Y  R  L  C  Q  V  N  E  S  C  S  W  I  J
N  U  L  E  T  K  I  E  K  S  M  U  U  W  I  F  C  M  X  T
L  N  K  K  B  J  K  M  E  C  K  Y  X  A  H  O  C  B  T  R
U  A  I  B  F  E  K  A  S  U  O  V  D  V  K  S  O  S  A  E
M  I  I  V  Y  L  M  B  A  E  U  W  I  V  O  X  Y  N  L  Z
```

ASHER	SOUTH	AMERICAN
COLOMBIA	BRAZIL	PERU
EIGHTH	SON	JACOB
LEAH	HAPPY	DAUGHTERS
BLESSED		

BENJAMIN

During slavery we had the "Maroons", which in Latin means Wolf.

BENJAMIN

Genesis 49:27 - [27] Benjamin shall ravin as a wolf: in the morning he shall devour the prey, and at night he shall divide the spoil.

```
V O N I G H T P A O U J E Y E O S E M V
W P S G M O E Y H T G A C M C Y J I M R
U W V N S R E Z E E V C S E D Z R F E A
G M J R A P L W D D X O E V L L S Z V T
D G F G Y I O K I C L B N H Q V W X F I
W E P B B X D I V I D E J T Z J V M M Q
A J J I C S O N L Z X I Z J U J E D M M
X V B E N X B Y I A Q Q T V J S N H D U
B Y I W Q V B I G D N X L I S R W L Y T
A R H J R H X R X T O N L W H M B R X O
V Y A F A D E N E W J K H P A S H I J V
X E O R E D P I C E O Z C G L A F I V F
R G F A L B A M D L V V M R L Y J I M W
U H Y V B K C A S F A D P R Z Y K E V A
O A C I A M A J W T D M V Y W G K T X Q
V V I N Q C Z N E H Y B E V E F G B K X
E X F W E X W E Z K J X K R E R E M N T
D Y V L L O L B O P S H Y W J C P S S C
S D E I O P R C R I G H T P N K C E W O
N D N X M W U N W X L C K H X S W Q H U
```

BENJAMIN	WEST	INDIANS
JAMAICA	TWELFTH	SON
RIGHT	JACOB	SHALL
RAVIN	WOLF	DEVOUR
PREY	NIGHT	DIVIDE
SPOIL		

BENJAMIN

Deuteronomy 33:12 - [12] And of Benjamin he said, The beloved of the LORD shall dwell in safety by him; and the Lord shall cover him all the day long, and he shall dwell between his shoulders.

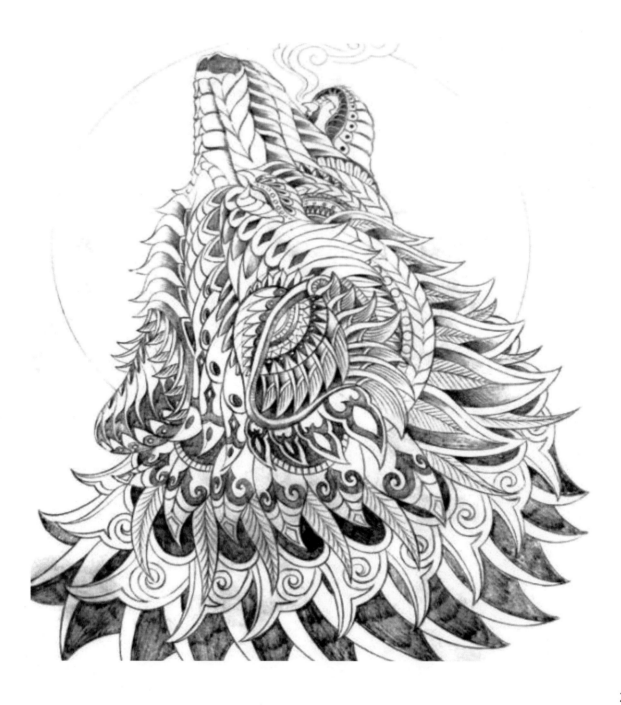

SIMEON

Levi was the 2nd son of Jacob. Is the so called Dominicans. Simeon means, "Afflicition heard".

Judah

Judah was the 4th born son of Jacob

Genesis 29:35 - ³⁵ And she conceived again, and bare a son: and she said, Now will I praise the LORD: therefore she called his name Judah; and left bearing.

EPHRAIM

Genesis 41:50-52 - [50] **And unto Joseph were born two sons before the years of famine came, which Asenath the daughter of Potipherah priest of On bare unto him.**
[51] **And Joseph called the name of the firstborn Manasseh: For God, said he, hath made me forget all my toil, and all my father's house.**

```
R C E X E X F U P P Q Q R A E Z P G H T
H A S S E N A M B Y L U F T I U R F I M
B P W P Q S T C T Y H K T Z X F T Y W Y
D T D J S R E O M R G L Q F S P J B H B
Z V X B N C Z E Z C P Q D A Y K D F A M
E J T S S M E Z T J C L Z J Q Y K J C H
T Q R A R O D K V H R W S O S N A B U C
S V E W D E D L A M P V N E R H P O F N
T E A Z U C E N X M R Q A S O M U X V G
W R R C A J D A T L O J C P Z P U L D B
D S B O R N K G Q D P N I H K R O V B M
T K Q X F X E P M N H A R S G L O R A Y
A O T F G G U K I O E S A C H V D D A S
K Y D E R E T T A C S V A R K F E A C U
H B A J R G Z S R E I S L V O D I G D Z
D H L T L K K S H S E H M R E Q L Z B H
G W O M J O N S P T D B G Q B E O K X E
Y T C G P G N N E M K E Q M Y C R X P V
V I E V G O N Z H U T P R O G K U R Y G
G I Z I H K C T X Y V P J M B O K T I Z
```

EPHRAIM	PUERTO	RICANS
SCATTERED	CUBANS	SECOND
BORN	JOESPH	FRUITFUL
MADE	FORGET	PROPHESIED
MANESSAH		

SIMEON

Genesis 49:6 [6] **O my soul, come not thou into their secret; unto their assembly, mine honour, be not thou united: for in their anger they slew a man, and in their selfwill they digged down a wall.**

EPHRAIM

Ephraim was the 2nd born of Joseph. Ephraim name means "I am fruitful".

They are the so called Puerto Ricans.

EPHRAIM

Genesis 48:14 - ¹⁴ And Israel stretched out his right hand, and laid it upon Ephraim's head, who was the younger, and his left hand upon Manasseh's head, guiding his hands wittingly; for Manasseh was the firstborn.

GAD

Deuteronomy 33:20 - [20] And of Gad he said, Blessed be he that enlargeth Gad: he dwelleth as a lion, and teareth the arm with the crown of the head.

```
L  S  J  O  Z  N  B  J  Y  X  C  O  M  W  T  X  Y  C  K  N
J  U  Y  W  V  P  G  D  U  G  N  X  T  B  B  F  M  O  Z  B
Z  H  Z  Y  S  O  I  U  H  N  V  B  E  M  R  Z  B  C  S  L
G  R  D  G  E  X  S  O  N  B  D  S  L  R  F  Y  O  O  O  E
J  S  J  M  Z  N  L  W  A  F  S  G  W  K  N  H  M  D  X  S
Q  G  B  Z  M  G  O  W  L  C  L  X  E  F  W  F  R  E  Z  S
B  M  G  M  I  R  J  I  A  R  Y  P  D  L  F  Z  X  G  N  E
E  E  V  I  C  V  O  T  L  C  G  A  P  L  Y  N  C  R  E  D
Q  M  F  P  E  I  T  O  D  W  E  L  L  E  T  H  X  A  R  P
Z  A  E  L  A  E  H  D  D  H  L  S  H  K  P  S  Y  L  W  H
V  N  W  D  R  U  J  T  N  B  U  J  B  N  U  E  V  N  Q  M
R  M  G  E  T  C  Z  Z  E  J  X  M  U  E  Z  K  T  E  Z  T
Z  J  D  S  H  Q  A  N  D  R  J  U  P  K  F  Q  Z  O  U  H
K  A  T  U  A  M  E  R  I  C  A  S  Q  Q  I  O  K  U  Q  S
N  C  E  P  J  C  Q  C  D  N  N  E  L  I  H  J  X  P  K  E
A  O  A  C  U  A  N  T  C  F  D  A  T  Z  M  N  V  O  G  V
X  B  T  A  R  L  B  W  F  B  L  I  V  R  V  D  O  O  C  E
U  P  L  M  T  H  V  A  H  X  K  G  A  D  P  F  T  R  C  N
X  R  K  W  V  O  A  C  D  E  Z  C  I  N  U  Z  A  T  T  T
Z  G  T  S  I  T  Y  X  R  E  J  P  R  V  S  I  Y  L  G  H
```

GAD	NORTH	AMERICA
INDIANS	SCATTERED	EARTH
SEVENTH	SON	JACOB
TROOP	NAME	BLESSED
ENLARGED	DWELLETH	LION
TEARETH	CROWN	HEAD

MANESSAH

Manessah was the first born son of Joseph. His name means "Made to Forget".
They are the so called Cubans.

MANESSAH

Genesis 41:51 - [51] **And Joseph called the name of the firstborn Manasseh: For God, said he, hath made me forget all my toil, and all my father's house.**

ZEBULON

ZEBULON was the 10th son of Jacob. His name means "My Dwelling". They are the so called Guatemala to Panama.

FILL IN THE MAP, WHERE ARE THE 12 TRIBES TODAY.

ZEBULON

Genesis 49:13 **13 Zebulun shall dwell at the haven of the sea; and he shall be for an haven of ships; and his border shall be unto Zidon.**

12 TRIBES CHART

```
P  I  Q  T  D  N  P  K  M  Z  R  R  N  H  Z  L  A  V  P  E
B  N  R  F  J  S  E  J  L  D  X  O  S  I  E  T  R  I  W  W
P  I  T  H  Q  C  N  C  P  X  E  P  E  R  F  A  W  M  T  N
E  M  G  B  L  Y  Y  Y  N  M  N  O  M  F  H  B  F  C  D  H
I  A  Y  J  B  W  K  I  I  V  L  A  W  C  L  P  V  P  I  O
D  J  T  E  J  G  A  S  H  E  R  Q  A  V  R  V  Y  K  H  O
A  N  I  T  H  A  U  N  X  I  G  S  W  Q  Y  B  T  I  H  C
Z  E  B  U  L  U  N  V  X  Y  S  I  T  U  G  Q  J  H  H  M
R  B  X  U  H  Z  Z  X  A  I  N  D  R  S  K  U  X  N  L  R
R  H  V  X  C  W  Q  D  U  L  K  A  P  R  C  M  E  F  J  X
D  J  O  J  C  D  J  E  F  F  X  Y  P  M  W  B  U  I  D  L
G  L  A  F  N  E  A  B  A  M  F  I  D  H  U  Z  S  J  W  Z
T  N  T  J  Z  J  P  D  Z  Y  C  T  H  E  T  P  Z  T  F  M
N  B  J  F  C  L  K  H  U  N  W  L  R  G  I  A  L  C  O  Q
I  W  M  V  X  I  A  Y  R  V  R  F  C  I  V  X  L  Q  R  F
Y  D  Z  J  G  D  D  Z  M  A  N  A  S  S  E  H  F  I  U  U
T  O  X  Q  U  F  E  Z  L  O  I  V  A  V  L  F  J  H  C  C
G  M  T  J  F  B  F  W  S  X  O  M  Y  N  P  P  D  V  G  J
T  M  F  E  U  R  B  K  C  Q  N  K  W  P  H  H  I  X  E  E
S  T  L  N  G  C  Y  K  D  Z  M  D  B  J  C  X  L  S  I  D
```

JUDAH	REUBEN	GAD
ASHER	NAPHTALI	MANASSEH
SIMEON	LEVI	ISSACHAR
ZEBULUN	BENJAMIN	EPHRAIM

ZEBULON

Deuteronomy 33:18 [18] And of Zebulun he said, Rejoice, Zebulun, in thy going out; and, Issachar, in thy tents.

REUBEN

REUBEN was the 1st born son of Jacob. His name means "See it's a Son". They are the so called Seminole and Muskogee Indians.

REUBEN

Genesis 29:32 ³² And Leah conceived, and bare a son, and she called his name Reuben: for she said, Surely the LORD hath looked upon my affliction; now therefore my husband will love me.

SIMEON

Genesis 29:33 - [33] **And she conceived again, and bare a son; and said, Because the LORD hath heard I was hated, he hath therefore given me this son also: and she called his name Simeon.**

```
V  Z  N  T  X  H  Y  H  L  S  O  S  E  R  C  F  U  F  J  H
G  W  J  B  K  E  U  L  S  N  K  N  E  C  A  D  A  T  A  N
M  Q  U  A  M  D  L  Q  C  E  Q  T  Y  W  P  O  F  T  Y  R
O  V  C  D  D  R  V  W  U  I  G  P  T  R  F  W  E  G  G  I
B  N  P  N  O  I  T  C  I  L  F  F  A  K  J  D  B  H  U  F
W  N  E  M  U  X  I  O  J  V  S  V  I  J  G  J  O  D  C  O
Z  G  K  M  B  U  T  B  D  X  C  L  L  D  N  O  C  E  S  G
Y  W  C  I  L  B  U  P  E  R  X  B  B  B  X  V  A  G  H  W
S  R  J  T  A  V  O  W  R  R  S  C  G  M  N  S  J  B  D  D
S  G  K  W  G  O  E  Z  E  S  F  K  D  F  O  L  C  U  B  Y
B  F  E  F  D  S  I  G  T  P  S  T  O  Y  K  A  O  K  T  N
V  V  Z  R  S  V  I  L  T  U  P  R  M  K  K  M  N  R  T  C
D  W  T  A  O  O  S  B  A  K  D  Y  I  I  S  C  C  B  D  D
S  D  L  O  N  R  I  W  C  C  G  N  O  O  O  E  I  T  Z
H  O  J  S  O  I  S  K  S  J  F  Y  I  M  H  F  I  X  T  J
U  M  K  P  E  V  E  H  G  M  H  R  C  G  W  S  V  L  O  Q
L  E  H  P  M  P  N  H  X  Y  R  N  A  Y  I  M  E  U  C  K
S  W  N  P  I  P  E  X  M  W  G  V  N  E  O  X  D  V  B  V
P  S  E  C  S  M  G  M  P  X  S  L  S  T  Z  N  E  V  I  G
D  L  D  E  Q  M  Q  I  C  C  R  M  Z  G  E  A  R  T  H  G
```

SIMEON	DOMINICANS	REPUBLIC
SCATTERED	REGIONS	EARTH
AFFLICTION	JACOB	SECOND
SON	GENESIS	CONCEIVED
LORD	HATED	GIVEN

NAPHTALI

Genesis 49:21 - [21] **Naphtali is a hind let loose: he giveth goodly words.**

REUBEN

Genesis 49:3 ³ Reuben, thou art my firstborn, my might, and the beginning of my strength, the excellency of dignity, and the excellency of power:

ASHER

ASHER was the eighth born son of Jacob. His name means "Happy". He is the so called Colombia, Brazil, Peru, Uruguay and Guyana.

ASHER

Genesis 30:13 [13] **And Leah said, Happy am I, for the daughters will call me blessed: and she called his name Asher.**

MANESSAH

Genesis 48:14 - [14] And Israel stretched out his right hand, and laid it upon Ephraim's head, who was the younger, and his left hand upon Manasseh's head, guiding his hands wittingly; for Manasseh was the firstborn.

```
Z  X  Z  G  R  D  R  W  L  Z  S  C  L  O  N  S  N  G  Y  S
D  S  V  L  H  Z  K  X  N  U  H  J  B  D  A  I  V  O  H  C
M  J  R  J  A  M  J  N  S  V  F  L  O  K  Y  T  G  E  E  A
F  G  L  O  S  W  M  Z  U  N  D  T  R  I  B  E  S  G  E  T
P  C  I  P  S  N  A  C  I  R  H  P  I  W  J  P  G  D  C  T
H  C  J  Z  E  Z  U  V  H  D  L  N  M  U  N  S  Q  I  H  E
S  S  D  S  N  O  I  T  A  R  G  I  M  H  R  E  J  W  G  R
M  I  N  R  A  F  M  E  O  R  V  T  U  X  S  F  B  Q  K  E
P  A  O  A  M  N  D  P  R  M  H  G  Y  E  K  C  M  N  K  D
O  L  C  K  B  E  I  H  A  T  J  H  H  J  Z  G  T  X  L  G
N  Y  E  P  V  U  P  R  X  X  W  P  T  Y  S  D  R  G  A  E
M  U  S  K  C  Q  C  A  I  W  R  S  I  T  L  E  W  G  G  N
K  J  S  S  D  U  G  I  V  O  K  E  P  B  M  T  R  Z  Q  E
B  G  F  S  W  N  U  M  P  O  B  O  U  D  N  Y  F  Z  O  S
R  T  W  E  L  V  E  H  V  R  O  J  E  A  V  D  N  T  Z  I
J  G  N  I  S  I  E  O  E  X  W  Q  R  F  O  R  G  E  T  S
D  V  W  S  W  S  Z  E  D  Y  M  B  T  G  N  W  H  V  E  S
Z  C  Z  A  I  Z  W  O  S  S  W  C  O  C  E  D  A  M  D  Q
R  N  C  E  U  R  K  T  T  R  M  B  C  R  I  U  P  P  I  I
E  X  D  Z  A  K  M  Y  J  W  B  Z  C  R  N  Q  T  C  D  M
```

EPHRAIM	PUERTO	RICANS
SCATTERED	CUBANS	SECOND
BORN	JOESPH	FRUITFUL
MADE	FORGET	PROPHESIED
MANESSAH	TRIBES	TWELVE
MIGRATION	GENESIS	

ASHER

Deuteronomy 33:24 **24 And of Asher he said, Let Asher be blessed with children; let him be acceptable to his brethren, and let him dip his foot in oil.**

ISSACHAR

ISSACHAR was the 9th born son of Jacob. His name means "He is Hired". They are the so called Mexicans.

USE THE SCRIPTURE TO FIND THE ANSWERS.

Across
2. NUMBERS 13:8
8. NUMBERS 13:14
9. NUMBERS 13:6
11. NUMBERS 13:11
12. NUMBERS 13:10

Down
1. NUMBERS 13:5
3. NUMBERS 13:4
4. NUMBERS 13:11
5. NUMBERS 13:7
6. NUMBERS 13:15
7. NUMBERS 13:9
10. NUMBERS 13:13

ISSACHAR

Genesis 49:14 - ¹⁴ Issachar is a strong ass couching down between two burdens:

Judah

JUDAH

Genesis 49:1 - 49 And Jacob called unto his sons, and said, Gather yourselves together, that I may tell you that which shall befall you in the last days.

```
Q  G  E  T  D  X  Y  X  K  C  J  Q  R  H  P  H  F  F  L  E
J  U  Q  M  E  Z  X  K  Z  E  M  H  C  E  G  A  T  H  A  N
J  E  S  P  R  J  L  F  D  K  L  R  I  M  K  D  H  N  E  L
P  Q  E  I  E  S  S  S  Z  I  B  Z  R  D  S  U  A  D  R  A
F  Z  Q  Z  T  E  V  T  H  S  W  D  W  E  L  J  U  Y  M  S
T  J  R  K  T  O  V  M  I  J  C  R  S  B  H  A  O  E  L  T
I  H  U  F  A  R  S  B  G  X  B  C  H  T  J  T  R  H  B  Q
V  D  T  H  C  G  H  S  F  C  L  K  M  Y  A  I  A  B  X  G
Y  O  U  R  S  E  L  V  E  S  L  D  T  N  C  W  G  G  S  Q
N  K  Q  Y  O  N  L  X  X  D  X  O  B  A  O  Y  U  G  B  M
F  R  A  K  V  N  G  L  J  N  G  O  N  J  B  C  C  W  Y  G
M  D  N  B  V  W  J  D  X  E  U  L  J  P  L  L  A  U  V  R
H  J  B  T  H  A  Z  F  T  A  C  D  S  B  X  D  V  L  S  I
F  F  E  C  E  T  F  H  A  Y  D  N  D  K  Z  V  R  A  C  O
U  C  F  Z  O  H  E  R  S  N  D  N  O  S  W  S  U  H  Z  D
O  O  A  P  Q  R  J  I  I  K  O  D  Z  S  I  W  O  I  X  B
C  A  L  L  E  D  B  T  A  C  C  U  Z  E  X  W  Y  T  K  V
S  O  L  V  P  C  L  M  L  H  A  A  P  B  B  R  L  B  O  T
V  A  U  E  J  L  K  X  I  C  W  N  L  T  F  E  A  L  K  L
T  M  B  A  T  C  O  K  J  H  E  H  M  B  U  B  L  F  R  V
```

JUDAH	AMERICAN	BLACKS
NEGROES	NORTH	SCATTERED
AFRICAN	JACOB	CALLED
SON	GATHER	YOURSELVES
TOGETHER	BEFALL	LAST
DAYS		

LEVI

LEVI is the 3rd son born of Jacob. His name means "Joined to me". They are the so called Haitians.

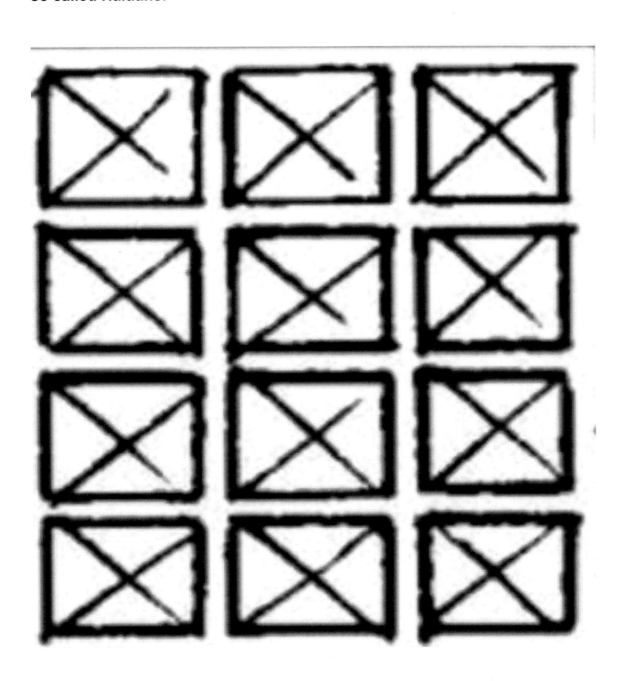

ISSACHAR

Deuteronomy 33:18 - [18] And of Zebulun he said, Rejoice, Zebulun, in thy going out; and, Issachar, in thy tents.

NAPHTALI

Deuteronomy 33:23King James Version (KJV)

23 And of Naphtali he said, O Naphtali, satisfied with favour, and full with the blessing of the LORD: possess thou the west and the south.

FIND YOUR TRIBE ON THIS MAP!!

NAPHTALI

LEVI

Genesis 29:34 - [34] And she conceived again, and bare a son; and said, Now this time will my husband be joined unto me, because I have born him three sons: therefore was his name called Levi.

TO BE
CONTINUED............

Made in United States
North Haven, CT
28 October 2021